I0541653

www.ingramcontent.com/pod-product-compliance
Lightning Source LLC
Chambersburg PA
CBHW041615120626
46551CB00002B/453

9798992918137

هَيَّا نَتَعَلَّم الأَشْكَال

Let's Learn Shapes

By Safa Adam

Welcome to Let's Learn Shapes!—a fun and interactive book designed to help young learners discover shapes in both English and Arabic.

Shapes are all around us, and learning them is an exciting first step in understanding the world. This book introduces children to basic shapes through colorful illustrations, simple words, and engaging activities. Each shape is presented in English and Arabic, making it a wonderful tool for bilingual families or anyone interested in introducing Arabic vocabulary in a natural way.

Dedication

To my beloved children,
-Ahmed, Salih, Noor, and Omer-
Love You
Safa

دَائِرَةٌ

Dayra

Circle

A ball is a circle

الكُرَةُ دَائِرَةٌ

Al-kura dayra

هَلْ تَسْتَطِيعُ أَنْ تَجِدَ دَوَائِرَ فِي الغُرْفَةِ؟

Can you find circles in the room?

مُرَبَّع

Mor-ab-ba'

Square

A window is a square

النَّافِذَةُ مُرَبَّعَةٌ

An-nafitha morabbah

اِتَّبِعِ المُرَبَّعَ بِإِصْبَعِكَ

Trace the square with your finger

مُثَلَّث

Mo-thal-lath

Triangle

A pizza slice is a triangle

قِطعَةُ البيتْزَا مُثَلَّثَة

Qit'at al-beitza muthallath

إِحْصِ الأَضْلَاعَ ١، ٢، ٣
Count the sides: 1, 2, 3

مُسْتَطِيلٌ

Mos-ta-teel

Rectangle

A door is a rectangle

اَلْبَابُ مُسْتَطِيلٌ

Al-bab mustateel

Which is longer: square or rectangle?

أَيُّهُمَا أَطْوَلُ: الْمُرَبَّعُ أَمِ الْمُسْتَطِيلُ؟

نَجْمَةٌ

Naj-ma

Star

A star in the sky

اَلنَّجْمَةُ فِي السَّمَاءِ

An-najma fi as-sama'

إِرْسُمْ نَجْمَةً فِي السَّمَاءِ

Draw a star in the sky

قَلْب

Qalb

Heart

Some leaves are hearts

بَعْضُ الأَوْرَاقِ عَلَى شَكْلِ قَلْب

Ba'd al-awraq 'ala shakl qalb

ضَعْ يَدَكَ عَلَى قَلْبِكِ

Put your hand on your heart!

بَيْضَوِيٌّ

Bay-da-wee

Oval

A melon is an oval

البَطِّيخَةُ بَيْضَوِيَّةٌ

Al-bateekha baydaweya

هَلِ البَيْضَوِيُّ يُشْبِهِ الدَّائِرَةَ؟ نَعَمْ أَمْ لَا؟

Does an oval look like a circle? Yes or no?

مُعِينٌ

Moa'-yin

Diamond

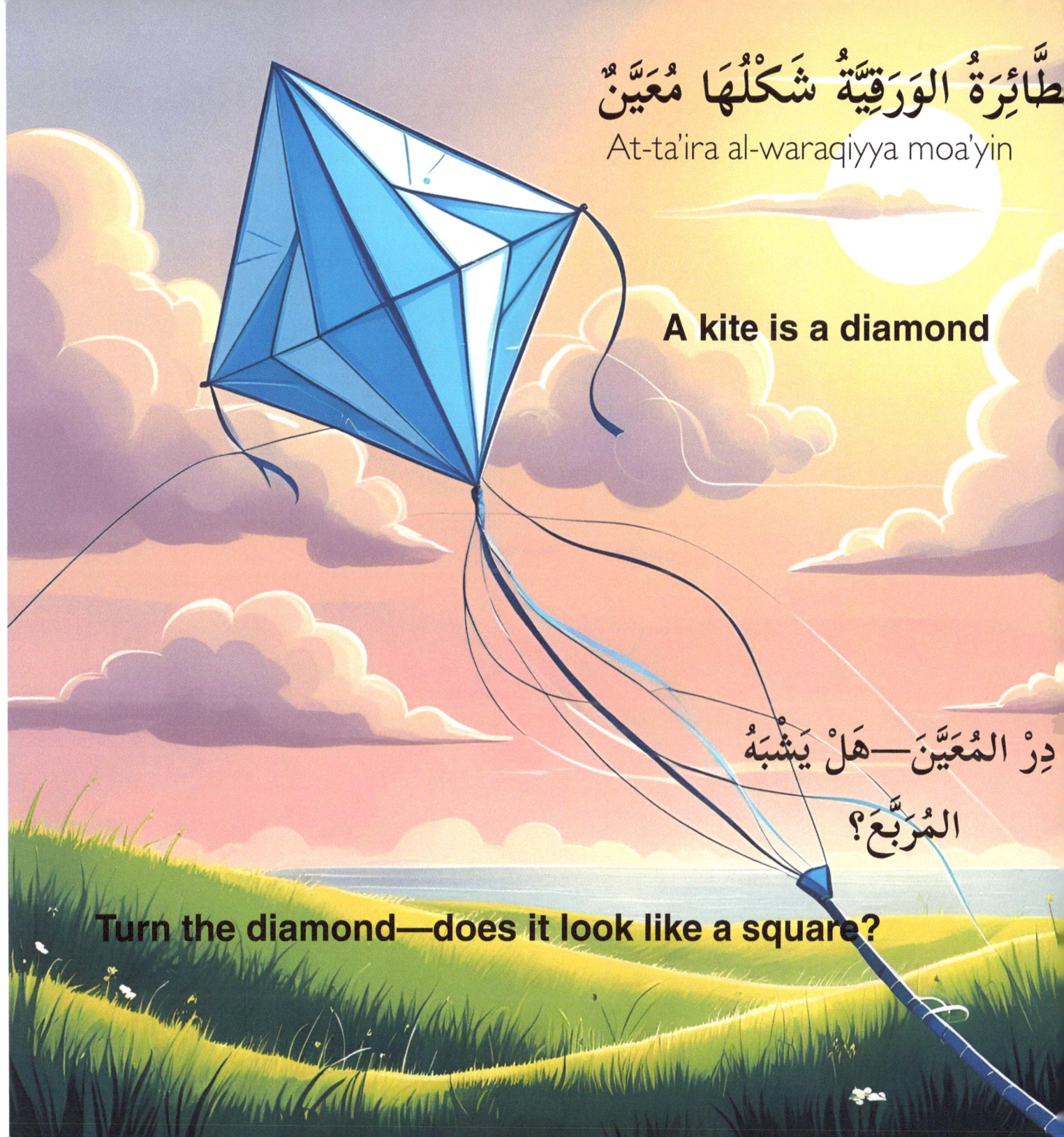

الطَّائِرَةُ الوَرَقِيَّةُ شَكْلُهَا مُعَيَّنْ

At-ta'ira al-waraqiyya moa'yin

A kite is a diamond

دِرْ المُعَيَّنَ—هَلْ يَشْبَهُ المُرَبَّعْ؟

Turn the diamond—does it look like a square?

هِلَالٌ

He-lal

Crescent

The moon is a crescent!

القَمَرُ هِلَالٌ

Al-qamar hilal

مَتَى تَرَى الهِلَالَ فِي السَّمَاءِ؟

When do you see a crescent moon?

Thank you for joining us on this journey of learning Arabic Shapes! We hope you and your little one enjoyed this book. Stay connected for more fun learning adventures!

P.S. I'd love to hear your thoughts! Email me at nooreenbooks@gmail.com

Design and layout by Safa Adam

First Edition: 2025

Self-Published by Safa Adam

ISBN: 979-8-9929181-3-7